Master Legal English

for Lawyers

English Writing, Grammar &
Punctuation for Law. Includes
Expert Legal Documents &
Templates

Copyright 2022

Topics Covered in this law book:
Legal writing, legal English, English for lawyers, grammar for lawyers, legal templates, law books for teens, law books for beginners, and law terminology book.

Contents

Introduction

Your writing is often the first and last impression you will leave in a professional interaction. While mastering it can open doors and make your path to success smoother, ignoring it can close doors and ruin potential opportunities for you. Your writing is too important to mess up when discussing legal and business matters.

In the legal world, different levels of communication take place, each one requiring different styles and approaches. For example, drafting contracts does not require the same approach as writing an email or an opinion. This book will help you not only write more professionally by understanding the nuts and bolts of English within legal contexts, but it will also help you decide when and how to use each tool.

"Know your context as well as your audience."

Like everything in life, not all writing is created equal. The same piece of writing can be a game-changing asset or a major liability, depending on when, where, and how we deploy it. We must always pay attention to context.

When you approach a piece of writing in a legal setting, the first thing to do is to decide exactly what you want from the exchange and what the context is. This is particularly important because you don't have the benefit of body language or facial expressions when you write. People tend to forget verbal exchanges more readily, but the written word is powerful.

"The pen is "mightier than the sword..." - Edward Bulwer-Lytton
and people will judge you based on how you use your pen.

About This Legal English Book

Master Legal English for Lawyers English Writing, Grammar & Punctuation for Law, provides a structured framework under which lawyers, law students, and other law professionals can significantly improve their knowledge of English to become more confident and effective writers.

You will be taken through the language structures that tend to create the most problems in the real world and encouraged to review them through highly targeted grammar exercises, which focus on developing your grammar skills and your competence and confidence in international legal communication.

The last section contains access to a large selection of templates to guide you through drafting contracts, letters, affidavits, and many other documents. It will be an invaluable resource for your studies and career in the legal arena.

Foreword

In my 10+ years of helping legal professionals improve their English communication skills, I've had the pleasure of working with some of the brightest, most driven people I have ever known. Some have become friends, and some have continued on their path with a friendly goodbye. I feel blessed to have had the chance to work with every one of them. This book is dedicated to them, without whom I would never have been able to come up with the ideas or inspiration to finish this project. This book aims to help legal professionals with:

- Legal Writing
- Essential Grammar
- Commonly Confused Language Structures that Cause the Most Problems in Real-World Scenarios
- Report Writing

- Proposal Writing
- Data Presentation
- General Legal
- Communication in English

Since English is the language used by many lawyers worldwide, this book aims to help those whose first language is not English and native English speakers who would just like a quick review of the basics. We are not focusing on specialized legal vocabulary here, but instead, we are homing in on the language structures that tend to cause the most issues in real-world scenarios. We will also focus on practicing and perfecting the basic building blocks of clear, professional communication within a legal context to gain the confidence you deserve. You will learn how to write clear, direct, and well-polished sentences so that you make a good impression in writing from the start.

This book contains key grammar and language guidelines to help you significantly improve your legal communication and avoid issues.

Contributors & Influencers

If you are interested in legal English Communication, I can recommend a few other books that will complement this one. At the risk of sounding like a fanboy, the following authors have written amazing books on the subject, and they deserve mention.

Although I cannot possibly list all the people who have influenced me through their work, I will try to mention a few of the ones who spring to mind in no particular order. These are my legal English communication heroes, and without their contribution through their work, I would never have been able to write this book.

If you have never read their books and are interested in Legal English Communication, I implore you to go out and buy them and read them over and over again.

Bryan A. Garner
Richard C. Wydick
William Strunk Jr.

Joel P. Trachtman
Antonin Scalia
Myron Magnet
Charles Murray

Get Entire Template Library
FOR FREE

Sign up for the no-spam newsletter and get an introductory book and more exclusive content, all for free.

Details can be found at the end of the book.

Why This Book?

This technical guide to the English language aims to help candidates on Bar Professional Training Courses, general law students, and law professionals.

A large part of the day-to-day work that legal professionals have to do centers around writing. A lawyer who receives a poorly written opinion may hesitate to send further work to the writer. Therefore, the need for good writing cannot be overlooked.

"Lawyers who use plain language know it doesn't just make good sense; it makes good cents."

Christopher Balmford, Words and Beyond, Australia

English for Lawyers will transform your legal communication skills with simple lessons and enjoyable activities to boost your writing, confidence, and performance.

Building advanced level Legal English requires more than gimmicks and set phrases *English for Lawyers*, aims to be straightforward, with easy lessons, to help transform you into a clear and confident communicator within legal settings. As mentioned earlier, the focus of this book is on the basic language structures that tend to cause the most issues within a legal context, not vocabulary.

The whole point of grammatical and syntactical rules is that the same structures should mean the same to the writer and the reader. This guidebook should not be read as a complete presentation of the 'rules' of English. We will be focusing instead on the main mistakes which cause the most issues for lawyers and other legal professionals in their day-to-day communication.

With this Legal English book, you can expect to:

- improve your legal writing and speaking
- feel more confident (particularly when you have to write to colleagues and clients)
- boost your performance and general efficiency at work through better writing
- lower your general stress levels by communicating clearly and correctly.

Legal English
Communication in Use

*"The language of the law
must not be foreign to the
ears of those who are to obey
it."*
Learned Hand

Subtle Persuasion

Laws and contracts aside, whether you like it or not, much of your day-to-day legal communication is about selling. 'Selling' can be defined as using communication to influence your reader or listener into taking some form of decision or action. So, it includes pretty much ANYTHING that you will ever write or speak about in your professional and even personal life.

- When you write an email to a boss, employee, or team member trying to influence them into taking a specific action, you're selling.
- When you write an email to an existing client trying to negotiate a better deal, you're selling.
- When you write the weekly newsletter, you're selling.

- You're selling when you post about yourself or your business on social media.
- The list goes on and on...

This section is about subtly persuading through language. Therefore, it is critical that you know precisely WHAT desired action you want your audience to take BEFORE you start writing.

Split Infinitives

Avoiding split infinitives originally comes from Latin, where you cannot split an infinitive verb (to + verb) since it is considered one word for all intents and purposes.

Although English is largely Latin-based, it is arguably slightly more flexible than the Romance languages, so we often include an adverb between "to" and the verb to clarify what we mean in certain situations or add to the flow of a sentence.

There used to be a strict rule against using split infinitives, but nowadays, even the Oxford English Dictionary allows for the use of split infinitives to avoid "awkward, stilted sentences." (1)

(1) Guardian Newspaper, *"To boldly go for it: why the split infinitive is no longer a*

mistake," The Guardian Online, Sep 25th, 2017

Examples of split infinitives:
*to **really** see*
*to **actually** be*
*to **finally** launch a venture*
*to **overtly** support*
*to **gradually** decrease*
*to **more than** double*

How Can Splitting Infinitives Help My Communication?

Sometimes, we need to split an infinitive to stop our sentences from being ambiguous or avoid sounding clumsy.

Exercise
What is the difference in meaning between these three sentences?
Which one should you use?

*A) "The parties agreed to **quickly** dissolve the contract."*

*B) "The parties **quickly** agreed to dissolve the contract."*

*C) "The parties agreed to dissolve the contract **quickly**."*

Answers

Question 1

A) "The parties agreed to **quickly** dissolve the contract."

This sentence refers to the speed with which the contract was to be dissolved.

B) "The parties **quickly** agreed to dissolve the contract."

This sentence refers to the speed with which the parties were able to come to an agreement.

C) "The parties agreed to dissolve the contract **quickly**."

The sentence is slightly unclear. We can't be 100% sure whether the adverb "quickly" describes how the parties agreed or how the contract would be dissolved. It also looks slightly clumsy, and there's no emphasis on "quickly." It almost looks like it's been included as an afterthought.

Question 2

This is a trick question since it depends on the meaning you want to express. Options 1 and 2 are preferable.

Can I split Infinitives in Legal Writing?

Generally speaking, it's best to avoid splitting infinitives in the legal world, as it is considered bad style in formal writing, and splitting infinitives is not usually necessary when referring to factual matters.

There may be some instances where you can use a split infinitive when you are being general or vague.

For example, *We expect investment in this area to almost triple over the next decade.* This, however, is not strictly legal English, as it is more business-related.

Exercise

Unsplit these infinitives without changing the meaning of the sentence. You can reorder or rewrite the sentence if needed.

We expect the number of investors in this area to almost triple over the next five years.

\-

The plaintiff failed to properly allege damages.

\-

Answers

We expect the number of investors in this area to increase/rise/grow by almost 300% over the next five years.

The plaintiff failed to allege damages properly.

Subject-Verb Agreement

The subject of any sentence we write must coincide with the verb form we use. If the doer of the action in our sentence is plural, then the verb must be written in its plural form. The same applies the other way, so if the doer of the action is singular, then the verb form must also be singular.

For example:
"**_The writ_** of execution **_was_** canceled."
"**_The accounts were_** forged."

Collective Nouns

In American English, collective nouns are treated as singular entities.

Example: "The **_team is_** losing all **_its_** players to injury."

Collective nouns can be treated as singular or plural in British English, though most British writers will gravitate towards the plural form.

Example: "*The **team are** losing all **their** players to injury.*"

Another example might be:
"*The **gift deeds were** submitted six days ago.*"
VS.
"*The **file with the gift deeds was** submitted six days ago.*"

This seems straightforward, but there can be issues when the collective noun is less clear.

Exercise:

Why is there a grammatical difference between *'a file'* and *'a number of'* or *'several'*? They are both collective nouns that refer to more than one individual within that collective. So, why the difference? Read the following two sentences and think about your answer. When you are ready, check your answer under the Answer section.

Sentence 1: *"The **file with the gift deeds was** submitted six days ago."*

VS.

Sentence 2: *"**Several gift deeds were** submitted six days ago."*

Answer:

In Sentence 1, the focal point of the message is 'the file.' We submitted the file, and there is only one file, so it's singular. However, in Sentence 2, the focus is on 'the deeds.' This is `plural.

This answer might be frustrating to some readers, as there are many nuances that can change the grammar of a sentence in English.

To go one step further and illustrate this, let's look at the following example:

"The **_number of gift deeds_** we drafted last year **_was_** much higher."

Exercise:

Why is 'the number of' suddenly singular?

We are still referring to more than one deed, so why is it now being treated as singular? Look at both sentences and think about your answer. When you are ready, check the Answer section.

Sentence 2: "A _**number of gift deeds were**_ submitted six days ago."

Sentence 3: "The _**number of gift deeds**_ we drafted last year _**was**_ much higher."

Answer:

The answer to this is the focus once more. Sentence 2, as we saw, focuses on the plurality of the deeds. Meanwhile, Sentence 3 focuses on the change to 'the number.' Was the number higher or lower? It was higher. If we focus on the change to this number, we need to treat it as singular because it's a singular number.

It's also worth noting that some nouns can be treated as singular or plural depending on preference.

Example:
Charity
Private Limited Company
Public Limited Company

Option 1: *Alpha Beta Charlie PLC* **are producers** *of free-range animal products.*

VS.

Option 2: *Alpha Beta Charlie PLC* **is a producer** *of free-range animal products.*

Both the above options are 100% correct. However, since a company is considered a separate individual legal entity, the norm is to express these nouns in the singular when discussing legal matters.

When referring to nouns like:
✓ Prosecution
✓ Jury
✓ Corporation

We can choose whether we write about them in singular or plural. The important thing is to remain consistent. We must choose a practice and stick to it as much as possible, especially within the same document.

Mixture of Singular and Plural Nouns

In the following example, several forms were sent to the NY office.
Therefore, we use the plural:

*"The non-disclosure agreement, the corporate bylaws, and the purchase agreement **were** all sent to our New York office on 23rd March."*

However, if we rewrite this sentence to focus the reader's attention on one particular document:

*"The non-disclosure agreement **was** sent to our New York office, **together with** corporate bylaws and the purchase agreement on 23rd March."*

The sentence's subject is now the *non-disclosure agreement,* so the verb needs to be singular.

When the subject of the sentence is an 'indefinite pronoun,' like the word *'each,'* we treat it as singular.

For example: *"**Each** of the forms **has** been filled out and sent to the relevant office."*

Sentences with Two Subjects

If the two subjects are singular, the verb stays singular:

*"Neither the <u>employment contract</u> nor the <u>loan agreement</u> **were** sent on time."*

Should be written as:
*"Neither the <u>employment contract</u> nor the <u>loan agreement</u> **was** sent on time."*

If one of the subjects is plural, we use a plural verb.
*"Neither the <u>employment contract**s**</u> nor the <u>loan agreement</u> **were** sent on time."*

*"Neither the <u>employment contract</u> nor the <u>loan agreement**s**</u> **were** sent on time."*

Verbs Versus Nouns

When we turn a base verb into a noun, this is called "nominalization." While it is very useful when we want to add variety to our professional writing, it can sometimes affect the power and meaning of our sentences.

Very noun-heavy sentences tend to be more watered-down in meaning since verbs carry more urgency and power.

They are also less direct and longer, sometimes making them convoluted.

Examples:

*The court **made the decision to grant** an injunction against Sean McFarlane after careful consideration.*

*The court **granted** an injunction against Sean McFarlane after careful consideration.*

The second sentence is better since it's clearer, more direct, and shorter.

Key Word Transformation Exercise:

The following sentences are quite noun-heavy and would be better expressed more directly. Transform them to make them clearer and more concise.

The considerable increase in crime over the past year has led to pressure being put on the police force (for a solution).

_____

The removal of the ambiguities in the contract made it look much clearer.

_____

Answers

Crime has increased considerably over the past year, and the police force is under pressure to find a solution.

The ambiguities in the contract were removed, which made it much clearer.

Ending a Sentence with a Preposition

This traditional guideline also comes from a rule used in Latin, where it is grammatically incorrect and nonsensical to end any sentence with a preposition. In many Romance languages, putting a preposition at the end of a sentence can make it unintelligible in many cases.

In English, on the other hand, it depends on the audience. Some readers adhere to this guideline strictly and, in some cases, will judge your writing to be sloppy if you end a sentence with a preposition. Therefore, if we are writing for a more traditional audience, we might want to avoid ending our sentences with prepositions.

Examples:
Option 1: Ending with a preposition

Advantages: More relaxed, direct, and clearer sentences.

Disadvantage: Might be judged poorly by some more traditional readers.

Example: *She is one of the few secretaries he enjoys working with.*

Option 2: Restructuring your sentence to avoid ending with a preposition

Advantages: Much more formal. It will satisfy more traditional readers.

Disadvantage: It depends on the type of writing. It can be quite impersonal in some cases, like in semi-formal emails to colleagues or clients. It is not as direct and clear as ending with a preposition in most cases.

Example: *She is one of the few secretaries with whom he enjoys working.*

The Problem with Obsessing Over the Preposition Guideline

English isn't Latin and is not structured in the same way as Italian, Spanish, etc. Therefore, the rules that apply there aren't always fully transferable to English.

When we speak, we do not always know how we will end our sentences. There are idioms and phrasal verbs in English that require the speaker or the writer to end some sentences with prepositions. This is not imposed by artificial, arbitrary rules; it's a requirement of real-world communication. It's important to remember that this is exactly what a language is designed to do. English is and should always be a constantly evolving tool for effective, purposeful communication. If we abandon this primary goal, we start to lose sight of what is important. As Winston Churchill once said, *"Correcting my grammar is something up with which I will not put."*

Punctuation

The Comma

Commas are designed to signal natural breaks or pauses within sentences and lists. However, they can also be placed following an introductory clause.

For example:
"Although the judge stated that she understood the defendant's difficult position, she denied bail due to the flight risk that he posed."

We can also use commas to add extra information in the middle of the sentence. Instead of using brackets, we can add two commas to separate the clause.

For example: *"Mr. Bryan A. Garner's email, which clearly stated the terms of the agreement, was received by Mr. Antonio Soprano on 15th May 2021."*

instead of

"Mr. Bryan A. Garner's email (which clearly stated the terms of the agreement) was received by Mr. Antonio Soprano on 15th May 2021."

Commenting Clauses VS Defining Clauses

'Commenting clauses' add extra information to a sentence while 'defining clauses' literally define whom we are referring to. We use commas to add extra background information with commenting clauses, but we omit the commas when using a defining clause to clarify whom we are talking about.

Example of a commenting clause:

"Mr. J. Pinkman, who was on probation at the time, drove to 308 Negra Arroyo Lane with a briefcase containing 10,000 USD in unmarked bills on the morning of March 6th, 2013."

Example of a defining clause:

"The company that presented the tender informed us that they were no longer in the position to offer us the service."

Here is an example of how this rule can change the meaning of your messages:

"As Mr. Wydick informed us, all set up costs incurred by new small businesses, who do not qualify for financial assistance from the IRS, can be covered using an interest-free loan from Trachtman Bank Ltd."

The commas mean that *'who do not qualify'* is a commenting

clause, adding extra background information about *'new small businesses.'* The sentence says that no new small businesses qualify for financial assistance from the IRS.

We can't add commas to the clause to communicate that some small businesses do not qualify for assistance.

"As Mr. Wydick informed us, all set up costs incurred by new small businesses who do not qualify for financial assistance from the IRS can be covered using an interest-free loan from Trachtman Bank Ltd."

The meaning in this second example is completely different. We have now used a 'defining clause' that specifies the type of new small businesses we are talking about. In this sentence, we are only talking about new small businesses that do not qualify for assistance, not those that do. As you can see, this is extremely important when it comes to writing within legal and business contexts.

Semicolons

We apply a semicolon (;) when we need to unite two closely related independent clauses (without conjunction). We add a comma to join two independent clauses closely related and separated by a conjunction.

Examples:
So, if our core message is:
The contract states that BDL Ltd. must inform XTZ Properties of all proposed building work at least 30 days prior to its approval, it does not specify who is responsible for paying for the administrative fees involved.

We can express it like this:
The contract states that BDL Ltd. must inform XTZ Properties of all proposed building work at least 30 days prior to its approval; **however,** *it does not specify who is responsible for paying for the administrative fees involved.*

While the word "However" is not needed in this particular example, we are using it to emphasize the connection between the two clauses and help our readers understand our message more clearly.

Another option would be to write:
The contract states that BDL Ltd. must inform XTZ Properties of all proposed building work at least 30 days prior to its approval, **but** *it does not specify who is responsible for paying for the administrative fees involved.*

"That" & "Which"

We use *"that"* to add a clause that defines exactly what we are talking or writing about. This clause should narrow the focus of the topic we are treating.

We use *"which"* to connect a clause that doesn't add extra focus on the discussion topic. This clause doesn't narrow down the topic.

Although *"that"* and *"which"* are often treated interchangeably in spoken English, when we are writing, our readers do not have the luxury of being able to infer meaning from our tone of voice and pauses. Therefore, it is vitally important that we pay attention to this rule.

The following two sentences illustrate the significance of using *"that"* and *"which"* correctly in writing:

Example 1: *The evidence **that** Mr. Miyagui presented to the judge was far from reliable.*

Meaning: This sentence means that of the larger body of evidence, the specific evidence presented by Mr. Miyagui wasn't reliable.

Example 2: *The evidence, **which** Mr. Miyagui presented to the judge, was far from accurate.*

Meaning: This sentence means that Mr. Miyagui presented all the evidence available, and it wasn't reliable.

As you can see, there is a huge difference in meaning here.

Conjunctions

As we looked at in the first book in this series, *Master Legal Vocabulary & Terminology*, we can connect two ideas or concepts in a single sentence, as long as we use the right conjunction. Conjunctions are essentially words that connect.

Look at the following example, which is missing a conjunction:
"The notice was served on 21 July, no response has been received."

How can you fix this sentence? Rewrite it below:

Answer:

The sentence would be better if we wrote it as follows:

*"The notice was served on 21 July, **but** no response has been received."*

In the answer above, the two parts of the sentence are linked by the conjunction **'but.'**

We could also start the sentence with '*although*':

Rewrite the sentence using the word '*although.*'

Answer:

*"**Although** the notice was delivered on 21 July, no response has been received."*

We can also express the same meaning using punctuation.

In the above example, we could use a **semicolon**:

Rewrite the sentence using a semicolon:

Answer:

"The notice was served on 21 July; no response has been received."

We can also use two sentences instead of one by using *'However'*:

Split the original sentence into two sentences using the word *'However.'*

Answer:

*"The notice was served on 21 July. **However,** no response has been received."*

Please Note: there should be a full stop or a semicolon in front of *'**however'*** if it introduces a new clause.

Ambiguous & Misused Modifiers

Words and groups of words that describe other words or groups of words are called 'modifiers.' We need to include any modifiers as closely as we can to the words they describe. Misplacing modifiers can lead to major misunderstandings and ambiguity.

Case Study: The Rule of the Last Antecedent

According to the last antecedent rule, if you add a modifier at the end of a list, this modifier only applies to the last item mentioned on that list.

For example:
"Trucks, motorbikes, and cars in New York." If we interpret this sentence literally, it refers to trucks and motorbikes from non-specific cities or regions. The only vehicles from New York we are referring to are the cars. This is extremely tricky because, in most written and spoken English, the communicator and the audience know that the trucks are from NY, the motorbikes from NY, and the cars from NY. It's implied in the sentence.

Lockhart v. U.S.

"The question presented: how to interpret statutory mandatory minimum sentences for sexual abuse. The result: a 6-2 split, broadly extending the statute's reach. The cause: a dangling modifier . . . ."

According to the statute, a ten-year mandatory minimum sentence should be applied to anyone with a prior conviction, who is then convicted of first-degree sexual abuse "relating to <u>aggravated sexual abuse</u>, <u>sexual abuse</u>, or <u>abusive</u>

<u>sexual conduct involving a minor or ward.</u>" https://www.lexisnexis.com/community/casebrief/p/casebrief-lockhart-v-united-states

According to the last antecedent rule, and most justices, the dangling modifier, 'involving a minor or ward,' could only be applied to abusive sexual conduct and not to the other offenses listed. In aggravated sexual abuse and sexual abuse cases, the victim didn't necessarily have to be underage to apply the ten-year mandatory minimum sentence.

The defendant, Avondale Lockhart, was caught in possession of child pornography and pleaded guilty. Mr. Lockhart had a prior conviction for sexual abuse of his adult girlfriend. This previous abuse of his adult girlfriend triggered the ten-year minimum sentence.

https://www.findlaw.com/legalblogs/supreme-court/the-supreme-court-comes-to-the-defense-of-the-dangling-modifier/

As stated above, we need to include any modifiers as closely as we can to the words they describe. Misplacing modifiers can lead to major misunderstandings and ambiguity. We often have to be extra-careful with one-word modifiers that limit the meaning of other words, like simply, exclusively, only, just, even, barely, nearly, or almost.

Exercise

What is the difference in meaning between these two sentences?

Option 1:

*Power issues **almost** led to 200 trains having to be canceled nationwide yesterday.*

Option 2:

*Power issues led to **almost** 200 trains having to be canceled nationwide yesterday.*

Answer:

Option 1:
Power issues almost led to 200 trains having to be canceled nationwide yesterday.

Meaning: The cancelations were narrowly avoided. The exact number of trains was 200.

Option 2:
Power issues led to almost 200 trains having to be canceled nationwide yesterday.

Meaning: The cancelations were not avoided, and almost 200 trains were canceled. It wasn't exactly 200 trains, the number was slightly lower, but we don't know exactly how many from the sentence.

Adding Descriptive Information with -ing phrases

We need to be careful not to complicate and distort our message when we add extra information using -ing verbs.

Exercise

Which sentence is clearer in meaning and easier to read? Why?

Option 1:
Sitting outside the courthouse, the client was updated on the current situation by the barrister.

Meaning: -------------------------------------

Option 2:
Sitting outside the courthouse, the barrister updated his client on the current situation.

Meaning: --------------------------------------

Answers:

Option 1:
Sitting outside the courthouse, the client was updated on the current situation by the barrister.

Meaning: Who was sitting outside the courthouse? The client? The barrister? Both? We don't know because it's not clear.

Option 2:
Sitting outside the courthouse, the barrister updated his client on the current situation.

Meaning: We know for certain that the barrister was outside the courthouse here. The client may have been there physically too or may have been on the phone, but the sentence is clear and organized. It conveys as much meaning as possible with fewer words.

Avoiding Common Mistakes in Legal English

What follows in this section is a review of some of the most problematic mistakes in Legal English. These are mistakes that both native and non-native English speakers often make, sometimes without ever realizing. To err is human, but if we want to give the best possible impression of ourselves in writing, we must keep our mistakes to a bare minimum. Please note that this is by no means an exhaustive list of possible errors but instead a handpicked selection of some of the most common ones.

How to Guide Your Audience's Attention

This section is all about how you can influence your reader's attention. Reading and listening are all about interpretation. How we interpret a message is influenced by many factors, but the focus of the message is one of the most important factors. We see this trick used every day in news headlines, bulletins, business reports, and even scientific papers. How the writer or speaker presents the ideas influences how we interpret the situation and the events. Use this technique wisely.

Eliminating Clutter

The lawyer's greatest weapon is clarity, and its whetstone is succinctness.
Judge Prettyman

When writing formally, many people's initial instinct is to clutter the beginning of a sentence with overly complicated yet unimportant language. However, if you make the reader's life harder by cluttering the beginning of your sentences, they will lose concentration. If you're trying to persuade, you need their attention, so keep sentences as simple as you can and aim to make a good impression at the beginning.

Example:
"According to a nationwide study carried out in 2019 by the National Institute of Statistics, 100,000 minors don't have access to adequate schooling."

This is OK, but if we want to focus the reader's attention on the fact that 100,000 minors don't have access to adequate schooling, it might be better if we write:

"100,000 minors don't have access to adequate schooling, according to a nationwide study carried out in 2019 by the National Institute of Statistics."

Manipulating Focus

Let's look at the same examples from above.

Example:

"According to a nationwide study carried out in 2019 by the National Institute of Statistics, 100,000 minors don't have access to adequate schooling."

As mentioned above, this is OK, but it would normally be better to focus the start of the sentence on the most important information, which is that 100,000 minors don't have access to adequate schooling UNLESS you aimed to draw attention away from this fact.

Compare them again:

"According to a nationwide study carried out in 2019 by the National Institute of Statistics, 100,000 minors don't have access to adequate schooling."

VS.

"100,000 minors don't have access to adequate schooling, according to a nationwide study carried out in 2019 by the National Institute of Statistics."

The first sentence takes some attention and, therefore, importance away from the fact that 100,000 minors don't have *adequate schooling.*

On the other hand, the second sentence makes it the prime focus. *100,000 minors don't have access to adequate schooling.* The secondary information about the study and when it was carried out takes a back seat and is therefore perceived as less relevant by the reader.

This simple trick is powerful, and it is something skilled writers and speakers know and implement all the time. The human mind focuses on the beginning of a sentence for important information. This is why when you read a sentence that starts with irrelevant information; your mind often switches off.

Before writing, get used to thinking about your objective.

What do you want the reader to focus on?

Put your most important words and concepts first or last, depending on your answer to this question.

Exercise 1:

Form sentences using the words provided. Write two versions for each sentence to switch the focus of the message, as shown in the example below. You can omit or add words if you think it will improve the sentence. Remember to focus on the message.

Example:

This/ material/mainly/ is/ used /car/ steering/ wheels/ of/ its/ durability /and/ light weight/ making/ because/ for

This material is mainly used for making car steering wheels because of its durability and light weight.

VS.

Because of its durability and light weight, this material is mainly used for making car steering wheels.

1. having/ this/ quarter/ are/ down/ last/ year/, despite/ the/ company/ had/ an/ increased/ and/ fewer/ overheads/ profits/ for/ workload/40%/ on/

_____

vs.

_____

2. 'Opening Doors to Women in Technology Award'/to /inform /you/ / earlier/ this week/ Claire Curtis/ joined/ our/ team/ in/ 2018/ as/ a/ technology/ consultant/ received/ the/ news/ that/ she/ has/ I/ am/ delighted/ been/shortlisted /for/ the

_____

VS.

_____

Exercise 2:

Transform each sentence to shift the focus of the message. You can change the order and the words used.

Example:

Initial investment is vital to the success of this project.

VS

The success of this project depends upon initial investment.

1. *Popular and cost-effective, this service should be added to our regular client package.*

2. *Key products are missing from this month's inventory*

3. The entire meeting was dedicated to discussing new business.

You can check your answers to exercises 1 and 2 on the next page.

Answers
Exercise 1:

1. having/ this/ quarter/ are/ down/ last/ year/, despite/ the/ company/ had/ an/ increased/ and/ fewer/ overheads/ profits/ for/ workload/40%/ on/

Profits for this quarter are down 40% on last year, despite the company having had an increased workload and fewer overheads.
VS.
Despite the company having had an increased workload and fewer overheads, profits for this quarter are down 40% on last year.

2. 'Opening Doors to Women in Technology Award'/to /inform /you/ / earlier/ this week/ Claire Curtis/ joined/ our/ team/ in/ 2018/ as/ a/ technology/ consultant/

**received/ the/ news/ that/
she/ has/ I/ am/ delighted/
been/shortlisted /for/ the**

*I am delighted to inform you that,
earlier this week, Claire Curtis,
who joined our team in 2018 as a
technology consultant, received
the news that she has been
shortlisted for the 'Opening
Doors to Women in Technology
Award.'
VS
Claire Curtis has been shortlisted
for the 'Opening Doors to
Women in Technology Award,' I
am delighted to inform you.
Claire joined our team in 2018 as
a technology consultant.*

Exercise 2:

1. *Popular and cost-effective, this service should be added to our regular client package.*

VS.
This service should be added to our regular client package, as it is popular and cost-effective.

2. *Key products are missing from this month's inventory*

VS.
This month's inventory is missing key products.

3. *The entire meeting was dedicated to discussing new business.*

VS.
Discussing new business was the focus of the entire

meeting.

Consistency in the Use of Terminology

Firstly, it's important to be consistent when using terminology, particularly when referring to the parties involved. This means being consistent in the names we use to identify things, places, companies, and people. Suddenly switching the label that we give to something in a document can lead to confusion, frustration, and even miscommunication. The writer must choose the label they will use and stick to it throughout the document.

For example: *'the organization,' 'the company,' 'XYZ PLC,' 'the defendant,' 'the respondent,' 'the employee,' 'the employer,'* etc.

Overly Elaborate Language

Contracts often contain extremely formal language, including words such as: *hereupon, herewith, hereafter, hereto, herein, hereby, hereof, hereunder, hereinbefore, hereinafter; thereafter, thereby, therein, thereinbefore, thereon, thereof, thereupon, thereunder, therewith; wherein, whereof, whereon, etc.*

- This type of language is not usually appropriate in emails or opinions.
- Statements of case should also be expressed in simpler English, with as little archaic language as possible.
- The writer should avoid using Latin and French if the word or phrase can be written in plain English.

Exercise:

Match the overly elaborate language 1-16, with its more direct, realistic equivalent, under the 'Realistic Equivalents' section.

1. Hereupon:
2. Herewith:
3. Herein:
4. Hereto:
5. Hereunder:
6. Hereof:
7. Hereafter:
8. Heretofore:
9. Herewith:
   10. Hereinafter:
   11. Hereby:
   12. Thereinafter:
   13. Thereinbefore:
   14. Therein:
   15. Thereafter:
   16. Aforementioned:

Realistic Equivalents

- after that
- from now on (for time)
- included from now on in this document.
- underneath this line
- previously mentioned.
- inside this document.
- together with this document
- included earlier in a document
- included in a document afterward.
- of this event/fact
- Following immediately after this (at this stage).
- Therefore
- Subsequently (afterward)
- inside that document
- related to this document
- previously (before this moment in time)

Check your answers on the next page.

Answers

1. Hereupon: Subsequently (afterward)
2. Herewith: Following immediately after this (at this stage).
3. Herein: inside this document.
4. Hereto: of this event/fact
5. Hereunder: underneath this line
6. Hereof: related to this document
7. Hereafter: from now on (for time)
8. Heretofore: previously (before this moment in time)
9. Herewith: together with this document
10. Hereinafter: included from now on in this document.
11. Hereby: therefore
12. Thereinafter: included in a document afterward.

13. Thereinbefore: included earlier in a document
14. Therein: inside that document
15. Thereafter: after that
16. Aforementioned: previously mentioned.

Here is a great article with some examples of words that you can eliminate: https://law.utexas.edu/faculty/wschiess/legalwriting/2008/06/ten-legal-words-and-phrases-we-can-do.html

Paragraphs

- Use the first sentence of each paragraph to outline the topic of the paragraph.
- Paragraphs with only one sentence are rarely appropriate.

- Long, complicated paragraphs are difficult and exhausting for readers.
- Separate topics always go in separate paragraphs. Do not fuse separate topics into one paragraph.
- Every paragraph should focus on one topic.
- You can often split long paragraphs into shorter paragraphs. When a topic is too large or complex for one paragraph, it should be split into several paragraphs.

"Who" vs. "Whom"

When a pronoun is the <u>subject</u> of a verb, we need to use "who."

Example: *Mr. Brown overheard Jack and Jill, **who** were talking about the contract.*

When a pronoun is the <u>object</u> of a verb or preposition, we use "whom."

.

Example: *Mr. Brown saw the man with* **whom** *Jill was talking about the contract.*

This rule has become more of a guideline for formal writing in modern English. It is acceptable to use "who" instead of "whom," but there will be readers who adhere strictly to the original rule and who will notice if we don't follow it exactly. Following this guideline can make our writing stiffer and less communicative. It may also make our sentences needlessly more complicated in some cases, but it will avoid potential issues with more traditional audiences.

Trick: If you can swap the word for *"he'"* or *"'she,"* use *"who."* If you can swap it for *"him"* or *"her,"* use *"whom."*

Standard Words & Phrases

Standard words and phrases that are often used incorrectly include the words:

'advice' noun VS *'advise'* verb.

'tortuous' VS' *tortious.'*

'counsel' (barrister) VS *'council'* (local authority).

'principle' (fundamental concept, or doctrine) VS *'principal'* (a person who employs an agent, etc.).

'Hone in on' vs. 'Home in on'

To *'home in on'* is when we direct our attention and focus toward something, or when our attention and focus are drawn to something.

Example:

The prosecution **homed in on** *the defendant's argument.*

One of the main meanings of "hone" is to sharpen or perfect something like a skill.

Example:

*The defendant **honed** her argument after the prosecution **homed in on** her claims that she did not understand the contract she had signed.*

Bibliography

Margot Costanzo, 'Legal Writing' (Cavendish Publishing Ltd, 1995)

J. M. Feinman, 'Law 101: Everything You Need to Know About American Law', Oxford University Press; 5th edition (August 8, 2018) https://www.amazon.com/Law-101-Everything-About-American/dp/0190866322/ref=sr_1_1?keywords=law+books+for+law+students&qid=1646824715&sprefix=law+books+%2Caps%2C409&sr=8-1

Bryan A. Garner, 'Black's Law Dictionary, 11th Edition', Thomson Reuters; 11th edition (June 10, 2019) https://www.amazon.com/Blacks-Dictionary-BLACKS-DICTIONARY-STANDARD/dp/1539229750/ref=sr_1_1?qid=1646825014&refinements=p_27

%3ABryan+A.+Garner&s=books&sr=
1-1&text=Bryan+A.+Garner

Bryan A. Garner, 'Legal Writing in
Plain English, Second Edition: A Text
with Exercises' (Chicago Guides to
Writing, Editing, and Publishing)
https://www.amazon.com/Legal-
Writing-Plain-English-
Second/dp/0226283933/ref=sr_1_4?
qid=1646825014&refinements=p_27
%3ABryan+A.+Garner&s=books&sr=
1-4&text=Bryan+A.+Garner

Guardian Newspaper, "To boldly
go for it: why the split infinitive is no
longer a mistake," *The Guardian
Online*, Sep 25th, 2017,
https://www.theguardian.com/scienc
e/shortcuts/2017/sep/25/to-boldly-
go-split-infinitive-grammatical-error-
research

Mary B. Ray & Jill J. Ramsfield,
'Legal Writing: Getting It Right and

Getting It Written' (3d ed. 2000).

Joel P. Trachtman, 'The Tools of Argument: How the Best Lawyers Think, Argue, and Win,' (2013) https://www.amazon.com/Tools-Argument-Lawyers-Think-Argue/dp/1481246380/ref=sr_1_1?crid=XD8PTOJUAQMF&keywords=law+books&qid=1646824389&sprefix=law+book%2Caps%2C341&sr=8-1

University of Chicago Press, The Chicago Manual of Style (1982).

Richard C. Wydick, Plain English for Lawyers (4th ed. 1998). https://www.amazon.com/Plain-English-Lawyers-Richard-Wydick/dp/153100699X/ref=sr_1_1?crid=2BBAESK56YO7N&keywords=Plain+English+for+Lawyers&qid=1646060136&sprefix=plain+english+for+lawyers%2Caps%2C372&sr=8-1

Writing Center (2003). *Ten Rules of Grammar and Usage that You Should Know*. Georgetown University Law Center https://www.law.georgetown.edu/wp-content/uploads/2018/07/grammar.pdf

William Zinsser, *On Writing Well: The Classic Guide to Writing,* Harper Perennial; Anniversary, Reprint edition (April 5, 2016) https://www.amazon.com/Writing-Well-Classic-Guide-Nonfiction/dp/0060891548

425 Legal Documents and Templates

Here, you will find a downloadable MS Word booklet with the 425 legal documents and templates, which you can use or edit as you please.
There is no need to sign up for our free resource newsletter, but if you do wish to receive more free resources, including free books and templates, please do not hesitate to sign up!

I hope you have found this book useful. Thank you for reading.
www.macsonbell.com/business-law-toolbox

Milton Keynes UK
Ingram Content Group UK Ltd.
UKHW022001130923
428636UK00005B/75

9 781806 315826